Perfectly Broken

Randolyn Allen

Presentation by *BookLeaf Publishing*

Web: www.bookleafpub.com

E-mail: info@bookleafpub.com

ISBN: 978-93-95890-02-1

First edition 2022

This book is dedicated to Morgan, Sean and Lena. My heart, my love, my soul.

ACKNOWLEDGEMENT

I would not be where I am today without the help of my father, Randy Allen, he is the most amazing man. He is a pillar of strength. He has a heart of gold and is the truest form of unconditional love. I hit the jackpot to be able to call him dad. He has provided, financial, emotional, and mental, support when I felt all was lost. He has never met a stranger and would give the shirt off his back to anyone in need. He is not only my father but also my hero.

PREFACE

Perfectly Broken is the story of a woman that once felt so broken. Broken beyond repair until she realized being perfectly broken made her someone she always longed to be. It was her Perfectly Broken moment that made her strong and love life like never before.

Life was Great

She was happy, comfortable and content
Years of marriage and just had her third child
The perfect mother and wife was her intent
The kids were free-spirited and perfectly wild
Worry and fear were hardly seen
Home all day enjoying her three
She let herself go and wasn't lean
Happiness was all she could see
Life was so perfect she felt like a queen

The Change

Her husband worked hard to provide
She was always begging for more time
She asked if he had something to hide
He got angry like she had committed a crime
In her eyes his job always came first
She tried the wrong way
Which always caused an outburst
She stupidly held on to hope each new day

The Reveal

Dark like any other night
He told her he was having an affair
After thirteen years there was a fight
She thought what they had was rare
The person she had been was now dead
He made choices and didn't care
She didn't want to get out of bed
Her heart and mind was broke
Feelings replaced with control, worry and fears
She realized he was wearing a cloke
To hide the person he truly was for years

Everyone

Everyone she loved so dear
Never liked him from the start
They all said to stay clear
She only listened to her heart
When the affair was told
She kept the secret from the world
Ashamed her heart grew cold
Her thoughts constantly swirled
The charade was hard to play
Her life was nothing social media portrayed
Darkness consumed her more each day
She could tell then she had been betrayed

Four Years of Lies

Four years she hide behind lies
Everyone believed their life was bliss
While her carefree spirit constantly dies
Her soul could not be fixed with a kiss
She spoke her truth to those so dear
The pain had already made its stain
Control, worry and fear
Was all she felt every single day
Her heart grew black
All she knew was to stay
Her old life was never coming back

Run Away

To make up for his choices
He moved the family from town to town
Control, worry and fear were her only voices
Each city just continued to bring her lies
She tried to control his actions
Everything she saw was not real in her eyes
She thought she was crazy
Her mind was constantly reliving the past
She was told she was lazy
She should have forgotten it fast
Just run away to a new city
New start a new path
She only felt pity
Relief was always found in the bath

When He Left

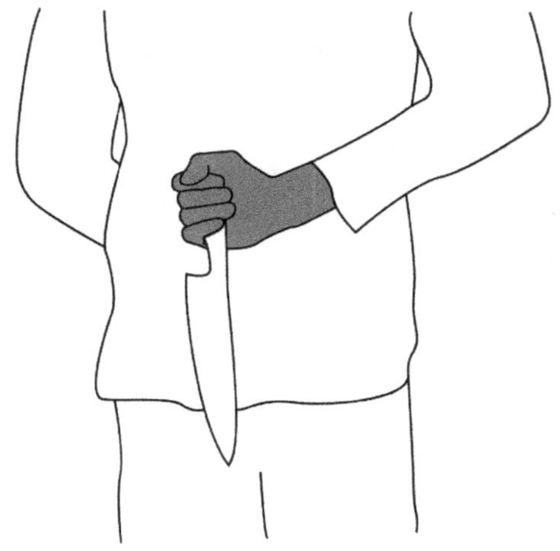

He was tired of the control
He wanted to live a free life
He had to complete his goal
He didn't want it with a wife
She was hurt and sad
She couldn't understand
How can he just leave, she was mad
She cried and finally took a stand
She was the one free
Free from the lies and deceit
After some time she could see
All was clear she would live a life on repeat

Self Love

Many months go by
It was long and hard
She grieved for the life she saw not the guy
She was able to let down her guard
Far too many years were given
She can't change the past
She is now living
She has found freedom that will last
No worry, control or fear
Truly happy she feels
The greatest things she holds dear
Her kids around her all day heals
The wound he created are no longer near

The Cycle

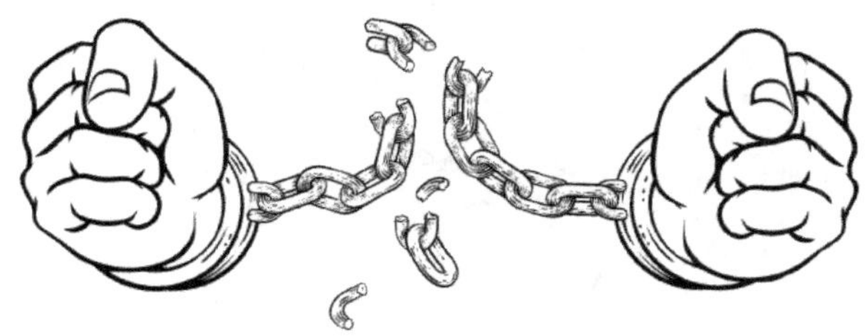

Self-love was one thing
Her thoughts were still her enemy
One moment his words would still sting
She was looking for her true identity
The good days lasted longer
Bad days her mind wanted to believe his lies
She had to face them to be stronger
Her past life didn't deserve her cries
But the cycle continued in her mind
She had to stop the self-torture
Her new life is what she had to find

New Life

She was set to start a new life
22 years played out in her mind
The words you were never meant to be a wife
So many words from the past unkind
She faced them head-on as they appeared
Each one was a brutal fear
Everything he said had to disappear
She knew who she was and that was clear
This new life she wanted was not going to be
easy

The Kids

In one moment was all it took
Her kids were so very happy
She had to dig deep to look
All she did was for them
Nothing in her life was ever for him
Her kids were her everything from the start
They are beautiful inside and out
They would always be the center of her heart
She was the one that raised them without a doubt

First Born

She is such a sensitive soul
Her heart is made of gold
She has so many gifts to achieve any goal
She has a love inside that will never fold
Her beauty is unmatched
Eyes like the ocean
All creatures she has the ability to be attached
Her mind sets everything in motion
Her love of all will always bring her peace
You are my heart and soul
I will always love you even after time will cease

The Son

He is a rock
Eyes as blue as the sky
His heart never has a lock
He gives his all to protect the ones he loves to
not cry
His intelligence is greater than he knows
Each day he grows
He will always take a stand
For what he believes is right
He is a collector
For the ones he loves he will put up a fight

He is a born protector
You are my simple man
I will always love you with all my heart even
after the ocean turns to sand

The Baby

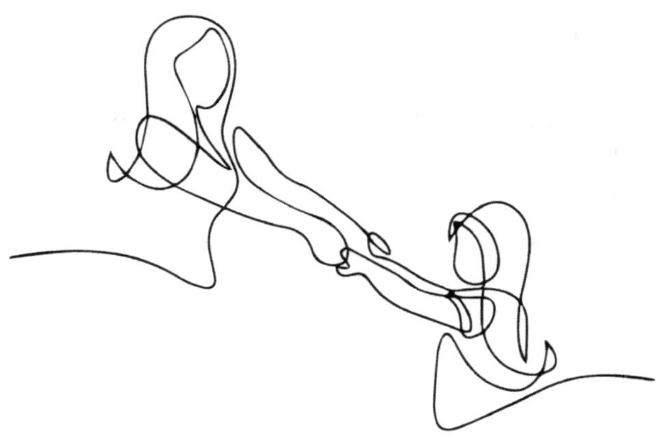

You have the eyes of your sister
The personality of your brother
The energy of a twister
You are like no other
You are so very beautiful
Very determined in all you do
No filter is very suitable
I hope you understand one day
I never want you to feel blue
I have been so protective
You are the baby
It's all I knew how to do
You are going to grow up one day
I always want you to stay true to you
So very smart
Food allergies have been hard
You are outgrowing them it's a start

We always had to be on guard
You are going to do so many great things
Always remember kindness and love is always
in sight
You are more powerful than all the kings
Your dreams are always within sight
I will always love you with all my heart for as
far as space and light

My Dad

My dad is my hero
His love for us is so true
To us he is a superhero
He is the reason we grew
He was always there for me
Tell me prayers and stories every night
When I was three
There was never a time he wasn't in sight
He is the reason I can be strong
He always told me to stall tall like a tree
He taught me to learn when I was wrong

He taught me the true meaning of being me
He makes friends everywhere he goes
One of the greatest souls
Everyone loves him that he knows
Thank you dad for being you

Time

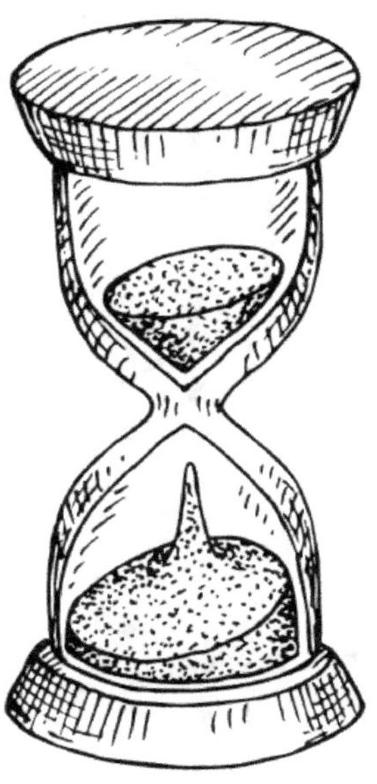

Time is so important to me
Every day I had with the ones I love
When they died I was able to see
Time was as precious as a dove
It cost nothing to give
It means everything to the one that gets it
When you don't get it it's hard to forgive
For some it is hard to admit
That time is all we have to control
The life I chose time will not be a regret
Time with my family has made me whole

Life Itself

Life is a mystery to me
So many things change
We do not see
So life has to rearrange
Good and bad is here for all
The way we responded is all we can control
Sometimes we fall
Into a deep dark hole
Sometimes we fly high on hope
One thing is for sure we can not mope
Nothing stays the same
Life is fun, sad, hopeful and plain
Remember it is just one big game

I Don't Know

I don't know what lies ahead
I'm not sure any of us do
Life is one day at a time instead
Whatever comes my way I will get through
Each moment is a blessing
I hope it is for you
Don't let life get to pressing
Don't let life get you blue
We all struggle with life
It's not just me or you
Don't allow it to cause strife
Each day can be made new